Networker's Tax and Expense Guide 2016

Richard Wayne Bobholz

Richard Wayne Bobholz

TABLE OF CONTENTS

Introduction

Congratulations on recognizing the importance of networking for your business! We are strong believers in the benefits of networking in building a business and have created this guide to help you make the most of your networking experience. There are many resources and books that describe the benefits of networking and how to network, so this guide is primarily going to showcase the tips and tricks every small business owner should know to save them money.

About our Authors

Richard Bobholz, managing partner at Law Plus Plus, works closely with his small business clients to handle all of their small business legal needs. He sets himself and his law firm apart by offering simplicity, expediency and exceptional work product. Bobholz values the relationship he has with his clients, allowing him to offer peace of mind through a more protective service. More information on Richard Bobholz, and Law Plus Plus, can be found at www.lawplusplus.com.

Instructions for Use

On the following pages, you will find the most current IRS approved deductions and credits for self-employed and W2 employees along with forms that help you keep track of these expenses.

Keeping detailed expense logs allows you to get the biggest bang for your buck at the end of the year. You shouldn't be taxed on expenses that otherwise would have been deducted; therefore, good records are critical.

Using this book will save you, or your accountant, a ton of time at the end of the year, and may illustrate deductions your accountant wouldn't have otherwise noticed without these detailed records. Your accountant can only find deductions that YOU provide information for.

Additionally, knowledge of these various deductions and credits will allow you to maximize your cash flow management so that you obtain beneficial tax treatment for activities and purchases you otherwise may have missed.

For any receipts or records that you record in this book, ensure that you keep these in a safe place for at least seven years, separated by year and by deduction category. For example, you should have a file or envelop titled "2016 Unreimbursed Employee Expenses."

If you have any questions or need help setting up the systems that go along with this book, you should contact your trusted accountant or CPA.

We strive to make all the things in this book as accurate and up to date as possible; however, this is merely a guidebook for educational purposes only. Nothing in this book is meant to be legal advice or tax advice. If you need legal advice, you should consult an attorney. If you need tax advice, you should consult your qualified tax professional.

IRS Circular 230 Disclosure: To ensure compliance with requirements imposed by the IRS, we inform you that any tax advice contained in this publication (including any attachments or web content) is not intended or written to be used by a client or any other person, and cannot be used, for the purpose of (i) avoiding penalties under the Internal Revenue Code or (ii) promoting, marketing, or recommending to another party any transaction or matter addressed herein.

In other words, do not rely on this publication for guidance through tricky legal or tax situations. This is meant simply to make you more aware of certain deductions and make it easier to keep track of those deductions.

Employees, S Corporations, C Corporations

Many of these deductions are not available unless you itemize if you are an employee, or the company you own is taxed as an S Corporation or C Corporation. You may want to consider a reimbursement plan through your company if you're taxed in any of these ways, as it could save you thousands of dollars each year in taxes.

Tip: The most important part of all of these deductions is documentation. Keep great records, or if that's not something you can easily do, hire someone to help. It will save you a lot of money.

Mileage and Automobile Expenses

For automobile costs, you have the choice of deducting the standard mileage deduction or portion of actual automobile expenses related to business.

The standard mileage deduction for 2016 is 54 cents. To receive this deduction, you must record every business mile you drive. See the attached mileage log for an easy way to keep track of these miles. The best way to do this is by keeping this book in your car or in the supplies you bring with you every day. If you have a briefcase, a purse, or a side pocket in your car door, these are all great places to keep this book.

The actual automobile expenses include all expenses you pay on an automobile that you are required to have for work, but only the proportion of each expense used for business purposes is allowable as a deduction. This can include the following:

1) Repairs and maintenance;
2) Licensing and DMV fees;
3) Parking and toll fees;
4) Loan payments;
5) Gas;
6) Garage rental fees; and
7) Insurance premiums.

Tip: With either method of deductions, you can deduct the cost of tolls and parking when business related.

Tip: You cannot use the standard mileage rate if: (1) you use five or more vehicles at the same time (such as fleet operations), (2) you claimed a depreciation deduction for the car using any method other than straight line, (3) you claimed a section 179 deduction on the vehicle, (4) you claimed the special depreciation allowance on the vehicle, (5) you claimed actual car expenses after 1997 for a car you leased, or (6) you are a rural mail carrier who received a qualified reimbursement.

Tip: Daily transportation expenses you incur while travelling from home to one or more regular places of business are generally non-deductible commuting expenses. Some exceptions include: (1) if you have one or more regular work locations away from your residence or (2) your residence is your principal place of business and you incur expenses going between the residence and another work location in the same trade or business.

Meals and Entertainment

You may be able to deduct business related entertainment and food expenses you incur for entertaining a client, customer, employee or other business connection. These deductions are heavily scrutinized and are subject to some tests. In order for them to be eligible deductions, the costs must be ordinary and necessary and meet either the Directly Related test or the Associated test as mandated by the IRS.

First and foremost, the expense must be ordinary and necessary. The expense is ordinary if it is the type that is commanded and accepted in your trade or business. The expenses are necessary if they are costs that are helpful and appropriate for your business. For example, the costs of a seminar on employment law put on by a lawyer would be ordinary and necessary because it is typical for lawyers to hosts seminars and a seminar would be helpful in building that lawyer's credibility as well as reaching more potential clients.

Next, the expense must pass the Directly Related Test or the Associated Test. In order for the expense to pass the Directly Related Test, you must show that (a) the main purpose of the combined business and entertainment was the active conduct of business, (b) you did engage in business with the person during the entertainment period, and (c) you had more than a general expectation of getting income or some other business benefit at some future time.

The expense passes the Associated Test if (a) entertainment is associated with your trade or business and (b) the entertainment is directly before or after a substantial business discussion.

Business Use of Home

Most small businesses start as a home business, and with that comes expenses that you should be recognizing as deductions on your tax return. Before you can claim deductions from the business use of your home, you must pass the tests set by the IRS.

The first test requires that (1) the business part of your home must be used exclusively and regularly for your trade or business, and (2) the business part of your home must be: (a) your principal place of business (second test), (b) a place where you meet or deal with patients, clients, or customers in the normal course of your trade or business, or (c) a separate structure used in connection with your trade or business.

To test if your home qualifies as your principal place of business, you must (1) use the office exclusively and regularly for administrative or management activities of your trade or business, and (2) you have no other fixed locations where you conduct substantial administrative or management activities of your trade or business.

If you're claiming to have your home office qualify as your principal place of business, you will need to pass both tests. Also note that the usage must be exclusively business. This means that you cannot claim your home office if you also use that space for personal use, like checking personal emails, watching TV, playing videogames, etc.

If you qualify, you can claim the home office deduction in one of two ways. Either you deduct $5 per square foot, up to $1,500 or you deduct the business portion of the following expenses:

1) Mortgage, rent or lease payments;
2) Telephone and fax expenses;
3) Internet expenses
4) Office supplies
5) Cell phone expenses;
6) Utilities;
7) Repairs and maintenance that affect the business portion; and
8) Professional services like cleaning, trash, and pest control.

At the end of the year, you would then take the total amount and multiply it by the percentage of square footage your home office space makes up of the home as a whole. For example, if you like in a 1,500 square foot house and your home office takes up 300 square feet, you would multiply the total by 20%.

> Tip: In order to gain the best tax benefit, you should keep track of all your expenses and determine at the end of the year which method to use.

Use the included schedule to help keep track of all of these costs.

Business Gifts

If your business gives out gifts around the holidays, rewards for a job well done or thank you gifts for your networking connections, you are entitled to use the business gifts deduction.

The IRS allows you to deduct no more than $25 per recipient per year for business related gifts. As an example, if you give $15 Starbucks gift cards to your best referral partners each quarter and end up giving 4 to the same person, you'd give $60 in value but are only allowed to deduct $25 of that.

Another type of business gift is the gift of entertainment. The IRS allows a deduction of up to 50% for gifts of entertainment, so you will likely get a much better deduction if you want to give a higher valued gift. Gifts of entertainment include things such as concert tickets, sporting event tickets, vacations and hotel costs.

Unreimbursed Employee Expenses

If you're a W2 employee, you're also entitled to your own specific deductions for out of pocket expenses that are not reimbursed by your employer. If the expense is reimbursed, you cannot lawfully claim the deductions.

In order to determine whether the expense incurred is deductible, it must be ordinary and necessary for your job. An ordinary expense is one that is common and accepted in your field of trade, business, or profession. A necessary expense is one that is helpful and appropriate for your business.

> Tip: A necessary expense does not have to be required to be considered necessary.

In order to take these deductions, you will use form 2106, or 2106-EZ if you qualify.

The IRS allows deductions for any expense that is ordinary and necessary for your job that was not reimbursed, so this commonly includes things like parking fees, uniforms, tolls, and business supplies.

There is one major limitation on what can be deducted. If you would have purchased this item for any other reason besides use at work, it is not deductible. For example, many people have tried to claim their suits as business expenses; however, because suits can be, and commonly are, used outside of work, they are not deductible under this deduction.

Tip: If you need specialized clothing that are specific to your industry, these will be deductible. i.e. work gloves, tool belt, protective wear.

Computers, Automobiles, and Capital Assets

Depreciation is an income tax deduction that allows a taxpayer to recover the cost or other basis of certain property over time. It is an annual allowance for the wear and tear, deterioration, or obsolescence of the property. Most types of tangible personal property such as buildings, machinery, vehicles, furniture and equipment are depreciable. Likewise, certain intangible property, such as patents, copyrights and certain licenses are also depreciable. In order to depreciate property, it must meet all of the following requirements:

1) You must own the property, or own the improvements to leased property;
2) You must use the property in business or an income producing activity (If used for personal and business, only the business portion may be depreciated);

3) The property must have a determinable useful life of more than one year; and
4) It cannot be of the following types of property:
    a. Property placed in service and disposed of in the same year;
    b. Equipment used to build capital improvements; and
    c. Certain term interests.

Depreciation begins the day you place the property in service for use in a trade, business or for the production of income. The property ceases to be depreciated when the taxpayer has fully recovered the property's depreciable value or when you retire the property from service, whichever happens first.

If you think you have assets that can be depreciated, speak with your CPA or bookkeeper to determine if and how you will depreciate the asset. This is not an area you will want to do yourself without training or extensive research beyond what this book can teach you.

General Tips on Networking

As you've probably already figured out, networking is about building relationships. We do that every day with our friends and our relatives, and the same principles apply to your business relationships as well. To that end, you should treat everyone you meet as though she is an important colleague or friend. Keeping this mindset will help you navigate many of the unpredictable networking situations you'll come across. For example, you would never approach a friend and try to convince him to buy from you. Instead, you'll want to see how your friend is doing and see if there is anything you can do to help him out.

Tip 1: Network to help others and they'll want to help you. If you network to give, not only will you be happier with the results, but those you help out will want to help you in return.

Tip 2: Never sell; instead, let your friends sell for you. If you have a good product or service, and you've established great working relationships, your colleagues will refer you business whenever they feel someone could benefit from what you have to offer.

Tip 3: Follow up. Never leave your colleague wondering where you went. Make her feel appreciated. The sooner you follow up, the better. Emails, phone calls and letters are all simple ways to reinforce your relationship with your colleague.

Tip 4: Introduce your new colleague to others within your network that might benefit from meeting with her. These people include her strategic partners as well as people who she might want to purchase products or services from. There's no point in having a strong network if you don't use it to help others out.

Tip 5: Smile. A good smile opens many doors.

Tip 6: Use this book and save money.

Schedule A – Automobile Expenses

Include in the description who the expense was paid to and, if helpful, how you paid (i.e. cash, credit card). Save all receipts.

Date	Expense Description	Amount

Automobile Expenses Continued...

Date	Expense Description	Amount

Schedule B - Business Use of Home

MONTH	Phone	Office Supply	Cell	Electric	Water	Gas	Repairs	Total
January								
February								
March								
April								
May								
June								
July								
August								
September								
October								
November								
December								

Schedule C – Mileage

Mileage Log	Vehicle _____
	Date ____/____/2016 to ____/____/2016

Date ____/____/2016	Total Miles _____
Odo Start _____	Odo End _____
From _____	To _____

Date ____/____/2016	Total Miles _____
Odo Start _____	Odo End _____
From _____	To _____

Date ____/____/2016	Total Miles _____
Odo Start _____	Odo End _____
From _____	To _____

Date ____/____/2016	Total Miles _____
Odo Start _____	Odo End _____
From _____	To _____

Date ____/____/2016	Total Miles _____
Odo Start _____	Odo End _____
From _____	To _____

Date ____/____/2016	Total Miles _____
Odo Start _____	Odo End _____
From _____	To _____

Date ____/____/2016	Total Miles _____
Odo Start _____	Odo End _____
From _____	To _____

Date ____/____/2016	Total Miles _____
Odo Start _____	Odo End _____
From _____	To _____

Date ____/____/2016	Total Miles _____
Odo Start _____	Odo End _____
From _____	To _____

Date ____/____/2016	Total Miles _____
Odo Start _____	Odo End _____
From _____	To _____

Date ____/____/2016	Total Miles _____
Odo Start _____	Odo End _____
From _____	To _____

Date ____/____/2016	Total Miles _____
Odo Start _____	Odo End _____
From _____	To _____
Date ____/____/2016	Total Miles _____
Odo Start _____	Odo End _____
From _____	To _____
Date ____/____/2016	Total Miles _____
Odo Start _____	Odo End _____
From _____	To _____
Date ____/____/2016	Total Miles _____
Odo Start _____	Odo End _____
From _____	To _____
Date ____/____/2016	Total Miles _____
Odo Start _____	Odo End _____
From _____	To _____
Date ____/____/2016	Total Miles _____
Odo Start _____	Odo End _____
From _____	To _____
Date ____/____/2016	Total Miles _____
Odo Start _____	Odo End _____
From _____	To _____
Date ____/____/2016	Total Miles _____
Odo Start _____	Odo End _____
From _____	To _____
Date ____/____/2016	Total Miles _____
Odo Start _____	Odo End _____
From _____	To _____
Date ____/____/2016	Total Miles _____
Odo Start _____	Odo End _____
From _____	To _____
Date ____/____/2016	Total Miles _____
Odo Start _____	Odo End _____
From _____	To _____

Date ____ / ____ /2016	Total Miles _____
Odo Start _____	Odo End _____
From _____	To _____
Date ____ / ____ /2016	Total Miles _____
Odo Start _____	Odo End _____
From _____	To _____
Date ____ / ____ /2016	Total Miles _____
Odo Start _____	Odo End _____
From _____	To _____
Date ____ / ____ /2016	Total Miles _____
Odo Start _____	Odo End _____
From _____	To _____
Date ____ / ____ /2016	Total Miles _____
Odo Start _____	Odo End _____
From _____	To _____
Date ____ / ____ /2016	Total Miles _____
Odo Start _____	Odo End _____
From _____	To _____
Date ____ / ____ /2016	Total Miles _____
Odo Start _____	Odo End _____
From _____	To _____
Date ____ / ____ /2016	Total Miles _____
Odo Start _____	Odo End _____
From _____	To _____
Date ____ / ____ /2016	Total Miles _____
Odo Start _____	Odo End _____
From _____	To _____
Date ____ / ____ /2016	Total Miles _____
Odo Start _____	Odo End _____
From _____	To _____
Date ____ / ____ /2016	Total Miles _____
Odo Start _____	Odo End _____
From _____	To _____

Date _____/_____/2016	Total Miles _____
Odo Start _____	Odo End _____
From _____	To _____
Date _____/_____/2016	Total Miles _____
Odo Start _____	Odo End _____
From _____	To _____
Date _____/_____/2016	Total Miles _____
Odo Start _____	Odo End _____
From _____	To _____
Date _____/_____/2016	Total Miles _____
Odo Start _____	Odo End _____
From _____	To _____
Date _____/_____/2016	Total Miles _____
Odo Start _____	Odo End _____
From _____	To _____
Date _____/_____/2016	Total Miles _____
Odo Start _____	Odo End _____
From _____	To _____
Date _____/_____/2016	Total Miles _____
Odo Start _____	Odo End _____
From _____	To _____
Date _____/_____/2016	Total Miles _____
Odo Start _____	Odo End _____
From _____	To _____
Date _____/_____/2016	Total Miles _____
Odo Start _____	Odo End _____
From _____	To _____
Date _____/_____/2016	Total Miles _____
Odo Start _____	Odo End _____
From _____	To _____
Date _____/_____/2016	Total Miles _____
Odo Start _____	Odo End _____
From _____	To _____

Date ____/____/2016	Total Miles _____
Odo Start _____	Odo End _____
From	To
Date ____/____/2016	Total Miles _____
Odo Start _____	Odo End _____
From	To
Date ____/____/2016	Total Miles _____
Odo Start _____	Odo End _____
From	To
Date ____/____/2016	Total Miles _____
Odo Start _____	Odo End _____
From	To
Date ____/____/2016	Total Miles _____
Odo Start _____	Odo End _____
From	To
Date ____/____/2016	Total Miles _____
Odo Start _____	Odo End _____
From	To
Date ____/____/2016	Total Miles _____
Odo Start _____	Odo End _____
From	To
Date ____/____/2016	Total Miles _____
Odo Start _____	Odo End _____
From	To
Date ____/____/2016	Total Miles _____
Odo Start _____	Odo End _____
From	To
Date ____/____/2016	Total Miles _____
Odo Start _____	Odo End _____
From	To
Date ____/____/2016	Total Miles _____
Odo Start _____	Odo End _____
From	To

Date	_____/_____/2016	Total Miles	_____
Odo Start	_____	Odo End	_____
From		To	

Date	_____/_____/2016	Total Miles	_____
Odo Start	_____	Odo End	_____
From		To	

Date	_____/_____/2016	Total Miles	_____
Odo Start	_____	Odo End	_____
From		To	

Date	_____/_____/2016	Total Miles	_____
Odo Start	_____	Odo End	_____
From		To	

Date	_____/_____/2016	Total Miles	_____
Odo Start	_____	Odo End	_____
From		To	

Date	_____/_____/2016	Total Miles	_____
Odo Start	_____	Odo End	_____
From		To	

Date	_____/_____/2016	Total Miles	_____
Odo Start	_____	Odo End	_____
From		To	

Date	_____/_____/2016	Total Miles	_____
Odo Start	_____	Odo End	_____
From		To	

Date	_____/_____/2016	Total Miles	_____
Odo Start	_____	Odo End	_____
From		To	

Date	_____/_____/2016	Total Miles	_____
Odo Start	_____	Odo End	_____
From		To	

Date	_____/_____/2016	Total Miles	_____
Odo Start	_____	Odo End	_____
From		To	

Date	_____/_____/2016	Total Miles	_____
Odo Start	_____	Odo End	_____
From		To	

Date _____/_____/2016	Total Miles _____
Odo Start _____	Odo End _____
From _____	To _____
Date _____/_____/2016	Total Miles _____
Odo Start _____	Odo End _____
From _____	To _____
Date _____/_____/2016	Total Miles _____
Odo Start _____	Odo End _____
From _____	To _____
Date _____/_____/2016	Total Miles _____
Odo Start _____	Odo End _____
From _____	To _____
Date _____/_____/2016	Total Miles _____
Odo Start _____	Odo End _____
From _____	To _____
Date _____/_____/2016	Total Miles _____
Odo Start _____	Odo End _____
From _____	To _____
Date _____/_____/2016	Total Miles _____
Odo Start _____	Odo End _____
From _____	To _____
Date _____/_____/2016	Total Miles _____
Odo Start _____	Odo End _____
From _____	To _____
Date _____/_____/2016	Total Miles _____
Odo Start _____	Odo End _____
From _____	To _____
Date _____/_____/2016	Total Miles _____
Odo Start _____	Odo End _____
From _____	To _____
Date _____/_____/2016	Total Miles _____
Odo Start _____	Odo End _____
From _____	To _____

Date	/	/2016	Total Miles	
Odo Start			Odo End	
From			To	
Date	/	/2016	Total Miles	
Odo Start			Odo End	
From			To	
Date	/	/2016	Total Miles	
Odo Start			Odo End	
From			To	
Date	/	/2016	Total Miles	
Odo Start			Odo End	
From			To	
Date	/	/2016	Total Miles	
Odo Start			Odo End	
From			To	
Date	/	/2016	Total Miles	
Odo Start			Odo End	
From			To	
Date	/	/2016	Total Miles	
Odo Start			Odo End	
From			To	
Date	/	/2016	Total Miles	
Odo Start			Odo End	
From			To	
Date	/	/2016	Total Miles	
Odo Start			Odo End	
From			To	
Date	/	/2016	Total Miles	
Odo Start			Odo End	
From			To	
Date	/	/2016	Total Miles	
Odo Start			Odo End	
From			To	

Date _____/_____/2016	Total Miles _____
Odo Start _____	Odo End _____
From	To

Date _____/_____/2016	Total Miles _____
Odo Start _____	Odo End _____
From	To

Date _____/_____/2016	Total Miles _____
Odo Start _____	Odo End _____
From	To

Date _____/_____/2016	Total Miles _____
Odo Start _____	Odo End _____
From	To

Date _____/_____/2016	Total Miles _____
Odo Start _____	Odo End _____
From	To

Date _____/_____/2016	Total Miles _____
Odo Start _____	Odo End _____
From	To

Date _____/_____/2016	Total Miles _____
Odo Start _____	Odo End _____
From	To

Date _____/_____/2016	Total Miles _____
Odo Start _____	Odo End _____
From	To

Date _____/_____/2016	Total Miles _____
Odo Start _____	Odo End _____
From	To

Date _____/_____/2016	Total Miles _____
Odo Start _____	Odo End _____
From	To

Date _____/_____/2016	Total Miles _____
Odo Start _____	Odo End _____
From	To

Date _____ / _____ /2016	Total Miles _____
Odo Start _____	Odo End _____
From _____	To _____
Date _____ / _____ /2016	Total Miles _____
Odo Start _____	Odo End _____
From _____	To _____
Date _____ / _____ /2016	Total Miles _____
Odo Start _____	Odo End _____
From _____	To _____
Date _____ / _____ /2016	Total Miles _____
Odo Start _____	Odo End _____
From _____	To _____
Date _____ / _____ /2016	Total Miles _____
Odo Start _____	Odo End _____
From _____	To _____
Date _____ / _____ /2016	Total Miles _____
Odo Start _____	Odo End _____
From _____	To _____
Date _____ / _____ /2016	Total Miles _____
Odo Start _____	Odo End _____
From _____	To _____
Date _____ / _____ /2016	Total Miles _____
Odo Start _____	Odo End _____
From _____	To _____
Date _____ / _____ /2016	Total Miles _____
Odo Start _____	Odo End _____
From _____	To _____
Date _____ / _____ /2016	Total Miles _____
Odo Start _____	Odo End _____
From _____	To _____
Date _____ / _____ /2016	Total Miles _____
Odo Start _____	Odo End _____
From _____	To _____

Date	/	/2016	Total Miles	
Odo Start			Odo End	
From			To	

Date	/	/2016	Total Miles	
Odo Start			Odo End	
From			To	

Date	/	/2016	Total Miles	
Odo Start			Odo End	
From			To	

Date	/	/2016	Total Miles	
Odo Start			Odo End	
From			To	

Date	/	/2016	Total Miles	
Odo Start			Odo End	
From			To	

Date	/	/2016	Total Miles	
Odo Start			Odo End	
From			To	

Date	/	/2016	Total Miles	
Odo Start			Odo End	
From			To	

Date	/	/2016	Total Miles	
Odo Start			Odo End	
From			To	

Date	/	/2016	Total Miles	
Odo Start			Odo End	
From			To	

Date	/	/2016	Total Miles	
Odo Start			Odo End	
From			To	

Date	/	/2016	Total Miles	
Odo Start			Odo End	
From			To	

Date	/	/2016	Total Miles	
Odo Start			Odo End	
From			To	
Date	/	/2016	Total Miles	
Odo Start			Odo End	
From			To	
Date	/	/2016	Total Miles	
Odo Start			Odo End	
From			To	
Date	/	/2016	Total Miles	
Odo Start			Odo End	
From			To	
Date	/	/2016	Total Miles	
Odo Start			Odo End	
From			To	
Date	/	/2016	Total Miles	
Odo Start			Odo End	
From			To	
Date	/	/2016	Total Miles	
Odo Start			Odo End	
From			To	
Date	/	/2016	Total Miles	
Odo Start			Odo End	
From			To	
Date	/	/2016	Total Miles	
Odo Start			Odo End	
From			To	
Date	/	/2016	Total Miles	
Odo Start			Odo End	
From			To	
Date	/	/2016	Total Miles	
Odo Start			Odo End	
From			To	

Date	/	/2016	Total Miles	
Odo Start			Odo End	
From			To	
Date	/	/2016	Total Miles	
Odo Start			Odo End	
From			To	
Date	/	/2016	Total Miles	
Odo Start			Odo End	
From			To	
Date	/	/2016	Total Miles	
Odo Start			Odo End	
From			To	
Date	/	/2016	Total Miles	
Odo Start			Odo End	
From			To	
Date	/	/2016	Total Miles	
Odo Start			Odo End	
From			To	
Date	/	/2016	Total Miles	
Odo Start			Odo End	
From			To	
Date	/	/2016	Total Miles	
Odo Start			Odo End	
From			To	
Date	/	/2016	Total Miles	
Odo Start			Odo End	
From			To	
Date	/	/2016	Total Miles	
Odo Start			Odo End	
From			To	
Date	/	/2016	Total Miles	
Odo Start			Odo End	
From			To	

Date	___/___/2016	Total Miles	_____
Odo Start	_____	Odo End	_____
From		To	

Date	___/___/2016	Total Miles	_____
Odo Start	_____	Odo End	_____
From		To	

Date	___/___/2016	Total Miles	_____
Odo Start	_____	Odo End	_____
From		To	

Date	___/___/2016	Total Miles	_____
Odo Start	_____	Odo End	_____
From		To	

Date	___/___/2016	Total Miles	_____
Odo Start	_____	Odo End	_____
From		To	

Date	___/___/2016	Total Miles	_____
Odo Start	_____	Odo End	_____
From		To	

Date	___/___/2016	Total Miles	_____
Odo Start	_____	Odo End	_____
From		To	

Date	___/___/2016	Total Miles	_____
Odo Start	_____	Odo End	_____
From		To	

Date	___/___/2016	Total Miles	_____
Odo Start	_____	Odo End	_____
From		To	

Date	___/___/2016	Total Miles	_____
Odo Start	_____	Odo End	_____
From		To	

Date	___/___/2016	Total Miles	_____
Odo Start	_____	Odo End	_____
From		To	

Date _____/_____/2016	Total Miles _____
Odo Start _____	Odo End _____
From _____	To _____
Date _____/_____/2016	Total Miles _____
Odo Start _____	Odo End _____
From _____	To _____
Date _____/_____/2016	Total Miles _____
Odo Start _____	Odo End _____
From _____	To _____
Date _____/_____/2016	Total Miles _____
Odo Start _____	Odo End _____
From _____	To _____
Date _____/_____/2016	Total Miles _____
Odo Start _____	Odo End _____
From _____	To _____
Date _____/_____/2016	Total Miles _____
Odo Start _____	Odo End _____
From _____	To _____
Date _____/_____/2016	Total Miles _____
Odo Start _____	Odo End _____
From _____	To _____
Date _____/_____/2016	Total Miles _____
Odo Start _____	Odo End _____
From _____	To _____
Date _____/_____/2016	Total Miles _____
Odo Start _____	Odo End _____
From _____	To _____
Date _____/_____/2016	Total Miles _____
Odo Start _____	Odo End _____
From _____	To _____
Date _____/_____/2016	Total Miles _____
Odo Start _____	Odo End _____
From _____	To _____

Date	/	/2016	Total Miles	
Odo Start			Odo End	
From			To	

Date	/	/2016	Total Miles	
Odo Start			Odo End	
From			To	

Date	/	/2016	Total Miles	
Odo Start			Odo End	
From			To	

Date	/	/2016	Total Miles	
Odo Start			Odo End	
From			To	

Date	/	/2016	Total Miles	
Odo Start			Odo End	
From			To	

Date	/	/2016	Total Miles	
Odo Start			Odo End	
From			To	

Date	/	/2016	Total Miles	
Odo Start			Odo End	
From			To	

Date	/	/2016	Total Miles	
Odo Start			Odo End	
From			To	

Date	/	/2016	Total Miles	
Odo Start			Odo End	
From			To	

Date	/	/2016	Total Miles	
Odo Start			Odo End	
From			To	

Date	/	/2016	Total Miles	
Odo Start			Odo End	
From			To	

Date _____ / _____ /2016	Total Miles	_____
Odo Start _____	Odo End	_____
From _____	To	
Date _____ / _____ /2016	Total Miles	_____
Odo Start _____	Odo End	_____
From _____	To	
Date _____ / _____ /2016	Total Miles	_____
Odo Start _____	Odo End	_____
From _____	To	
Date _____ / _____ /2016	Total Miles	_____
Odo Start _____	Odo End	_____
From _____	To	
Date _____ / _____ /2016	Total Miles	_____
Odo Start _____	Odo End	_____
From _____	To	
Date _____ / _____ /2016	Total Miles	_____
Odo Start _____	Odo End	_____
From _____	To	
Date _____ / _____ /2016	Total Miles	_____
Odo Start _____	Odo End	_____
From _____	To	
Date _____ / _____ /2016	Total Miles	_____
Odo Start _____	Odo End	_____
From _____	To	
Date _____ / _____ /2016	Total Miles	_____
Odo Start _____	Odo End	_____
From _____	To	
Date _____ / _____ /2016	Total Miles	_____
Odo Start _____	Odo End	_____
From _____	To	
Date _____ / _____ /2016	Total Miles	_____
Odo Start _____	Odo End	_____
From _____	To	

Date	/	/2016	Total Miles	
Odo Start			Odo End	
From			To	

Date	/	/2016	Total Miles	
Odo Start			Odo End	
From			To	

Date	/	/2016	Total Miles	
Odo Start			Odo End	
From			To	

Date	/	/2016	Total Miles	
Odo Start			Odo End	
From			To	

Date	/	/2016	Total Miles	
Odo Start			Odo End	
From			To	

Date	/	/2016	Total Miles	
Odo Start			Odo End	
From			To	

Date	/	/2016	Total Miles	
Odo Start			Odo End	
From			To	

Date	/	/2016	Total Miles	
Odo Start			Odo End	
From			To	

Date	/	/2016	Total Miles	
Odo Start			Odo End	
From			To	

Date	/	/2016	Total Miles	
Odo Start			Odo End	
From			To	

Date	/	/2016	Total Miles	
Odo Start			Odo End	
From			To	

Date _____/_____/2016	Total Miles _____
Odo Start _____	Odo End _____
From _____	To _____

Date _____/_____/2016	Total Miles _____
Odo Start _____	Odo End _____
From _____	To _____

Date _____/_____/2016	Total Miles _____
Odo Start _____	Odo End _____
From _____	To _____

Date _____/_____/2016	Total Miles _____
Odo Start _____	Odo End _____
From _____	To _____

Date _____/_____/2016	Total Miles _____
Odo Start _____	Odo End _____
From _____	To _____

Date _____/_____/2016	Total Miles _____
Odo Start _____	Odo End _____
From _____	To _____

Date _____/_____/2016	Total Miles _____
Odo Start _____	Odo End _____
From _____	To _____

Date _____/_____/2016	Total Miles _____
Odo Start _____	Odo End _____
From _____	To _____

Date _____/_____/2016	Total Miles _____
Odo Start _____	Odo End _____
From _____	To _____

Date _____/_____/2016	Total Miles _____
Odo Start _____	Odo End _____
From _____	To _____

Date _____/_____/2016	Total Miles _____
Odo Start _____	Odo End _____
From _____	To _____

Date	___/___/2016	Total Miles	_____
Odo Start	_____	Odo End	_____
From		To	

Date	___/___/2016	Total Miles	_____
Odo Start	_____	Odo End	_____
From		To	

Date	___/___/2016	Total Miles	_____
Odo Start	_____	Odo End	_____
From		To	

Date	___/___/2016	Total Miles	_____
Odo Start	_____	Odo End	_____
From		To	

Date	___/___/2016	Total Miles	_____
Odo Start	_____	Odo End	_____
From		To	

Date	___/___/2016	Total Miles	_____
Odo Start	_____	Odo End	_____
From		To	

Date	___/___/2016	Total Miles	_____
Odo Start	_____	Odo End	_____
From		To	

Date	___/___/2016	Total Miles	_____
Odo Start	_____	Odo End	_____
From		To	

Date	___/___/2016	Total Miles	_____
Odo Start	_____	Odo End	_____
From		To	

Date	___/___/2016	Total Miles	_____
Odo Start	_____	Odo End	_____
From		To	

Date	___/___/2016	Total Miles	_____
Odo Start	_____	Odo End	_____
From		To	

Date _____/_____/2016	Total Miles _____
Odo Start _____	Odo End _____
From _____	To _____
Date _____/_____/2016	Total Miles _____
Odo Start _____	Odo End _____
From _____	To _____
Date _____/_____/2016	Total Miles _____
Odo Start _____	Odo End _____
From _____	To _____
Date _____/_____/2016	Total Miles _____
Odo Start _____	Odo End _____
From _____	To _____
Date _____/_____/2016	Total Miles _____
Odo Start _____	Odo End _____
From _____	To _____
Date _____/_____/2016	Total Miles _____
Odo Start _____	Odo End _____
From _____	To _____
Date _____/_____/2016	Total Miles _____
Odo Start _____	Odo End _____
From _____	To _____
Date _____/_____/2016	Total Miles _____
Odo Start _____	Odo End _____
From _____	To _____
Date _____/_____/2016	Total Miles _____
Odo Start _____	Odo End _____
From _____	To _____
Date _____/_____/2016	Total Miles _____
Odo Start _____	Odo End _____
From _____	To _____
Date _____/_____/2016	Total Miles _____
Odo Start _____	Odo End _____
From _____	To _____

Date _____ / _____ /2016	Total Miles _____
Odo Start _____	Odo End _____
From _____	To _____

Date _____ / _____ /2016	Total Miles _____
Odo Start _____	Odo End _____
From _____	To _____

Date _____ / _____ /2016	Total Miles _____
Odo Start _____	Odo End _____
From _____	To _____

Date _____ / _____ /2016	Total Miles _____
Odo Start _____	Odo End _____
From _____	To _____

Date _____ / _____ /2016	Total Miles _____
Odo Start _____	Odo End _____
From _____	To _____

Date _____ / _____ /2016	Total Miles _____
Odo Start _____	Odo End _____
From _____	To _____

Date _____ / _____ /2016	Total Miles _____
Odo Start _____	Odo End _____
From _____	To _____

Date _____ / _____ /2016	Total Miles _____
Odo Start _____	Odo End _____
From _____	To _____

Date _____ / _____ /2016	Total Miles _____
Odo Start _____	Odo End _____
From _____	To _____

Date _____ / _____ /2016	Total Miles _____
Odo Start _____	Odo End _____
From _____	To _____

Date _____ / _____ /2016	Total Miles _____
Odo Start _____	Odo End _____
From _____	To _____

Date _____/_____/2016	Total Miles	_____
Odo Start _____	Odo End	_____
From	To	
Date _____/_____/2016	Total Miles	_____
Odo Start _____	Odo End	_____
From	To	
Date _____/_____/2016	Total Miles	_____
Odo Start _____	Odo End	_____
From	To	
Date _____/_____/2016	Total Miles	_____
Odo Start _____	Odo End	_____
From	To	
Date _____/_____/2016	Total Miles	_____
Odo Start _____	Odo End	_____
From	To	
Date _____/_____/2016	Total Miles	_____
Odo Start _____	Odo End	_____
From	To	
Date _____/_____/2016	Total Miles	_____
Odo Start _____	Odo End	_____
From	To	
Date _____/_____/2016	Total Miles	_____
Odo Start _____	Odo End	_____
From	To	
Date _____/_____/2016	Total Miles	_____
Odo Start _____	Odo End	_____
From	To	
Date _____/_____/2016	Total Miles	_____
Odo Start _____	Odo End	_____
From	To	
Date _____/_____/2016	Total Miles	_____
Odo Start _____	Odo End	_____
From	To	

Date	/ /2016		Total Miles	
Odo Start			Odo End	
From			To	
Date	/ /2016		Total Miles	
Odo Start			Odo End	
From			To	
Date	/ /2016		Total Miles	
Odo Start			Odo End	
From			To	
Date	/ /2016		Total Miles	
Odo Start			Odo End	
From			To	
Date	/ /2016		Total Miles	
Odo Start			Odo End	
From			To	
Date	/ /2016		Total Miles	
Odo Start			Odo End	
From			To	
Date	/ /2016		Total Miles	
Odo Start			Odo End	
From			To	
Date	/ /2016		Total Miles	
Odo Start			Odo End	
From			To	
Date	/ /2016		Total Miles	
Odo Start			Odo End	
From			To	
Date	/ /2016		Total Miles	
Odo Start			Odo End	
From			To	
Date	/ /2016		Total Miles	
Odo Start			Odo End	
From			To	

Date _____ / _____ /2016	Total Miles _____
Odo Start _____	Odo End _____
From _____	To _____
Date _____ / _____ /2016	Total Miles _____
Odo Start _____	Odo End _____
From _____	To _____
Date _____ / _____ /2016	Total Miles _____
Odo Start _____	Odo End _____
From _____	To _____
Date _____ / _____ /2016	Total Miles _____
Odo Start _____	Odo End _____
From _____	To _____
Date _____ / _____ /2016	Total Miles _____
Odo Start _____	Odo End _____
From _____	To _____
Date _____ / _____ /2016	Total Miles _____
Odo Start _____	Odo End _____
From _____	To _____
Date _____ / _____ /2016	Total Miles _____
Odo Start _____	Odo End _____
From _____	To _____
Date _____ / _____ /2016	Total Miles _____
Odo Start _____	Odo End _____
From _____	To _____
Date _____ / _____ /2016	Total Miles _____
Odo Start _____	Odo End _____
From _____	To _____
Date _____ / _____ /2016	Total Miles _____
Odo Start _____	Odo End _____
From _____	To _____
Date _____ / _____ /2016	Total Miles _____
Odo Start _____	Odo End _____
From _____	To _____

Date _____/_____/2016	Total Miles _____
Odo Start _____	Odo End _____
From	To
Date _____/_____/2016	Total Miles _____
Odo Start _____	Odo End _____
From	To
Date _____/_____/2016	Total Miles _____
Odo Start _____	Odo End _____
From	To
Date _____/_____/2016	Total Miles _____
Odo Start _____	Odo End _____
From	To
Date _____/_____/2016	Total Miles _____
Odo Start _____	Odo End _____
From	To
Date _____/_____/2016	Total Miles _____
Odo Start _____	Odo End _____
From	To
Date _____/_____/2016	Total Miles _____
Odo Start _____	Odo End _____
From	To
Date _____/_____/2016	Total Miles _____
Odo Start _____	Odo End _____
From	To
Date _____/_____/2016	Total Miles _____
Odo Start _____	Odo End _____
From	To
Date _____/_____/2016	Total Miles _____
Odo Start _____	Odo End _____
From	To
Date _____/_____/2016	Total Miles _____
Odo Start _____	Odo End _____
From	To

Date _____/_____/2016	Total Miles _____
Odo Start _____	Odo End _____
From _____	To _____

Date _____/_____/2016	Total Miles _____
Odo Start _____	Odo End _____
From _____	To _____

Date _____/_____/2016	Total Miles _____
Odo Start _____	Odo End _____
From _____	To _____

Date _____/_____/2016	Total Miles _____
Odo Start _____	Odo End _____
From _____	To _____

Date _____/_____/2016	Total Miles _____
Odo Start _____	Odo End _____
From _____	To _____

Date _____/_____/2016	Total Miles _____
Odo Start _____	Odo End _____
From _____	To _____

Date _____/_____/2016	Total Miles _____
Odo Start _____	Odo End _____
From _____	To _____

Date _____/_____/2016	Total Miles _____
Odo Start _____	Odo End _____
From _____	To _____

Date _____/_____/2016	Total Miles _____
Odo Start _____	Odo End _____
From _____	To _____

Date _____/_____/2016	Total Miles _____
Odo Start _____	Odo End _____
From _____	To _____

Date _____/_____/2016	Total Miles _____
Odo Start _____	Odo End _____
From _____	To _____

Date	/	/2016	Total Miles	
Odo Start			Odo End	
From			To	
Date	/	/2016	Total Miles	
Odo Start			Odo End	
From			To	
Date	/	/2016	Total Miles	
Odo Start			Odo End	
From			To	
Date	/	/2016	Total Miles	
Odo Start			Odo End	
From			To	
Date	/	/2016	Total Miles	
Odo Start			Odo End	
From			To	
Date	/	/2016	Total Miles	
Odo Start			Odo End	
From			To	
Date	/	/2016	Total Miles	
Odo Start			Odo End	
From			To	
Date	/	/2016	Total Miles	
Odo Start			Odo End	
From			To	
Date	/	/2016	Total Miles	
Odo Start			Odo End	
From			To	
Date	/	/2016	Total Miles	
Odo Start			Odo End	
From			To	
Date	/	/2016	Total Miles	
Odo Start			Odo End	
From			To	

Date	_____/_____/2016	Total Miles	_____
Odo Start	_____	Odo End	_____
From		To	

Date	_____/_____/2016	Total Miles	_____
Odo Start	_____	Odo End	_____
From		To	

Date	_____/_____/2016	Total Miles	_____
Odo Start	_____	Odo End	_____
From		To	

Date	_____/_____/2016	Total Miles	_____
Odo Start	_____	Odo End	_____
From		To	

Date	_____/_____/2016	Total Miles	_____
Odo Start	_____	Odo End	_____
From		To	

Date	_____/_____/2016	Total Miles	_____
Odo Start	_____	Odo End	_____
From		To	

Date	_____/_____/2016	Total Miles	_____
Odo Start	_____	Odo End	_____
From		To	

Date	_____/_____/2016	Total Miles	_____
Odo Start	_____	Odo End	_____
From		To	

Date	_____/_____/2016	Total Miles	_____
Odo Start	_____	Odo End	_____
From		To	

Date	_____/_____/2016	Total Miles	_____
Odo Start	_____	Odo End	_____
From		To	

Date	_____/_____/2016	Total Miles	_____
Odo Start	_____	Odo End	_____
From		To	

Date	_____/_____/2016		Total Miles	_____
Odo Start	_____		Odo End	_____
From			To	
Date	_____/_____/2016		Total Miles	_____
Odo Start	_____		Odo End	_____
From			To	
Date	_____/_____/2016		Total Miles	_____
Odo Start	_____		Odo End	_____
From			To	
Date	_____/_____/2016		Total Miles	_____
Odo Start	_____		Odo End	_____
From			To	
Date	_____/_____/2016		Total Miles	_____
Odo Start	_____		Odo End	_____
From			To	
Date	_____/_____/2016		Total Miles	_____
Odo Start	_____		Odo End	_____
From			To	
Date	_____/_____/2016		Total Miles	_____
Odo Start	_____		Odo End	_____
From			To	
Date	_____/_____/2016		Total Miles	_____
Odo Start	_____		Odo End	_____
From			To	
Date	_____/_____/2016		Total Miles	_____
Odo Start	_____		Odo End	_____
From			To	
Date	_____/_____/2016		Total Miles	_____
Odo Start	_____		Odo End	_____
From			To	
Date	_____/_____/2016		Total Miles	_____
Odo Start	_____		Odo End	_____
From			To	

Date ___/___/2016	Total Miles _____
Odo Start _____	Odo End _____
From _____	To _____
Date ___/___/2016	Total Miles _____
Odo Start _____	Odo End _____
From _____	To _____
Date ___/___/2016	Total Miles _____
Odo Start _____	Odo End _____
From _____	To _____
Date ___/___/2016	Total Miles _____
Odo Start _____	Odo End _____
From _____	To _____
Date ___/___/2016	Total Miles _____
Odo Start _____	Odo End _____
From _____	To _____
Date ___/___/2016	Total Miles _____
Odo Start _____	Odo End _____
From _____	To _____
Date ___/___/2016	Total Miles _____
Odo Start _____	Odo End _____
From _____	To _____
Date ___/___/2016	Total Miles _____
Odo Start _____	Odo End _____
From _____	To _____
Date ___/___/2016	Total Miles _____
Odo Start _____	Odo End _____
From _____	To _____
Date ___/___/2016	Total Miles _____
Odo Start _____	Odo End _____
From _____	To _____
Date ___/___/2016	Total Miles _____
Odo Start _____	Odo End _____
From _____	To _____

Date	____ / ____ /2016	Total Miles	_____
Odo Start	_____	Odo End	_____
From		To	
Date	____ / ____ /2016	Total Miles	_____
Odo Start	_____	Odo End	_____
From		To	
Date	____ / ____ /2016	Total Miles	_____
Odo Start	_____	Odo End	_____
From		To	
Date	____ / ____ /2016	Total Miles	_____
Odo Start	_____	Odo End	_____
From		To	
Date	____ / ____ /2016	Total Miles	_____
Odo Start	_____	Odo End	_____
From		To	
Date	____ / ____ /2016	Total Miles	_____
Odo Start	_____	Odo End	_____
From		To	
Date	____ / ____ /2016	Total Miles	_____
Odo Start	_____	Odo End	_____
From		To	
Date	____ / ____ /2016	Total Miles	_____
Odo Start	_____	Odo End	_____
From		To	
Date	____ / ____ /2016	Total Miles	_____
Odo Start	_____	Odo End	_____
From		To	
Date	____ / ____ /2016	Total Miles	_____
Odo Start	_____	Odo End	_____
From		To	
Date	____ / ____ /2016	Total Miles	_____
Odo Start	_____	Odo End	_____
From		To	

Date _____/_____/2016	Total Miles _____
Odo Start _____	Odo End _____
From _____	To _____

Date _____/_____/2016	Total Miles _____
Odo Start _____	Odo End _____
From _____	To _____

Date _____/_____/2016	Total Miles _____
Odo Start _____	Odo End _____
From _____	To _____

Date _____/_____/2016	Total Miles _____
Odo Start _____	Odo End _____
From _____	To _____

Date _____/_____/2016	Total Miles _____
Odo Start _____	Odo End _____
From _____	To _____

Date _____/_____/2016	Total Miles _____
Odo Start _____	Odo End _____
From _____	To _____

Date _____/_____/2016	Total Miles _____
Odo Start _____	Odo End _____
From _____	To _____

Date _____/_____/2016	Total Miles _____
Odo Start _____	Odo End _____
From _____	To _____

Date _____/_____/2016	Total Miles _____
Odo Start _____	Odo End _____
From _____	To _____

Date _____/_____/2016	Total Miles _____
Odo Start _____	Odo End _____
From _____	To _____

Date _____/_____/2016	Total Miles _____
Odo Start _____	Odo End _____
From _____	To _____

Date	____/____/2016	Total Miles	_____
Odo Start	_____	Odo End	_____
From		To	
Date	____/____/2016	Total Miles	_____
Odo Start	_____	Odo End	_____
From		To	
Date	____/____/2016	Total Miles	_____
Odo Start	_____	Odo End	_____
From		To	
Date	____/____/2016	Total Miles	_____
Odo Start	_____	Odo End	_____
From		To	
Date	____/____/2016	Total Miles	_____
Odo Start	_____	Odo End	_____
From		To	
Date	____/____/2016	Total Miles	_____
Odo Start	_____	Odo End	_____
From		To	
Date	____/____/2016	Total Miles	_____
Odo Start	_____	Odo End	_____
From		To	
Date	____/____/2016	Total Miles	_____
Odo Start	_____	Odo End	_____
From		To	
Date	____/____/2016	Total Miles	_____
Odo Start	_____	Odo End	_____
From		To	
Date	____/____/2016	Total Miles	_____
Odo Start	_____	Odo End	_____
From		To	
Date	____/____/2016	Total Miles	_____
Odo Start	_____	Odo End	_____
From		To	

Date _____ / _____ /2016	Total Miles _____
Odo Start _____	Odo End _____
From _____	To _____
Date _____ / _____ /2016	Total Miles _____
Odo Start _____	Odo End _____
From _____	To _____
Date _____ / _____ /2016	Total Miles _____
Odo Start _____	Odo End _____
From _____	To _____
Date _____ / _____ /2016	Total Miles _____
Odo Start _____	Odo End _____
From _____	To _____
Date _____ / _____ /2016	Total Miles _____
Odo Start _____	Odo End _____
From _____	To _____
Date _____ / _____ /2016	Total Miles _____
Odo Start _____	Odo End _____
From _____	To _____
Date _____ / _____ /2016	Total Miles _____
Odo Start _____	Odo End _____
From _____	To _____
Date _____ / _____ /2016	Total Miles _____
Odo Start _____	Odo End _____
From _____	To _____
Date _____ / _____ /2016	Total Miles _____
Odo Start _____	Odo End _____
From _____	To _____
Date _____ / _____ /2016	Total Miles _____
Odo Start _____	Odo End _____
From _____	To _____
Date _____ / _____ /2016	Total Miles _____
Odo Start _____	Odo End _____
From _____	To _____

Date _____/_____/2016	Total Miles _____	
Odo Start _____	Odo End _____	
From _____	To _____	
Date _____/_____/2016	Total Miles _____	
Odo Start _____	Odo End _____	
From _____	To _____	
Date _____/_____/2016	Total Miles _____	
Odo Start _____	Odo End _____	
From _____	To _____	
Date _____/_____/2016	Total Miles _____	
Odo Start _____	Odo End _____	
From _____	To _____	
Date _____/_____/2016	Total Miles _____	
Odo Start _____	Odo End _____	
From _____	To _____	
Date _____/_____/2016	Total Miles _____	
Odo Start _____	Odo End _____	
From _____	To _____	
Date _____/_____/2016	Total Miles _____	
Odo Start _____	Odo End _____	
From _____	To _____	
Date _____/_____/2016	Total Miles _____	
Odo Start _____	Odo End _____	
From _____	To _____	
Date _____/_____/2016	Total Miles _____	
Odo Start _____	Odo End _____	
From _____	To _____	
Date _____/_____/2016	Total Miles _____	
Odo Start _____	Odo End _____	
From _____	To _____	
Date _____/_____/2016	Total Miles _____	
Odo Start _____	Odo End _____	
From _____	To _____	

Date	/	/2016	Total Miles	
Odo Start			Odo End	
From			To	

Date	/	/2016	Total Miles	
Odo Start			Odo End	
From			To	

Date	/	/2016	Total Miles	
Odo Start			Odo End	
From			To	

Date	/	/2016	Total Miles	
Odo Start			Odo End	
From			To	

Date	/	/2016	Total Miles	
Odo Start			Odo End	
From			To	

Date	/	/2016	Total Miles	
Odo Start			Odo End	
From			To	

Date	/	/2016	Total Miles	
Odo Start			Odo End	
From			To	

Date	/	/2016	Total Miles	
Odo Start			Odo End	
From			To	

Date	/	/2016	Total Miles	
Odo Start			Odo End	
From			To	

Date	/	/2016	Total Miles	
Odo Start			Odo End	
From			To	

Date	/	/2016	Total Miles	
Odo Start			Odo End	
From			To	

Date	_____ / _____ /2016	Total Miles	_____
Odo Start	_____	Odo End	_____
From		To	
Date	_____ / _____ /2016	Total Miles	_____
Odo Start	_____	Odo End	_____
From		To	
Date	_____ / _____ /2016	Total Miles	_____
Odo Start	_____	Odo End	_____
From		To	
Date	_____ / _____ /2016	Total Miles	_____
Odo Start	_____	Odo End	_____
From		To	
Date	_____ / _____ /2016	Total Miles	_____
Odo Start	_____	Odo End	_____
From		To	
Date	_____ / _____ /2016	Total Miles	_____
Odo Start	_____	Odo End	_____
From		To	
Date	_____ / _____ /2016	Total Miles	_____
Odo Start	_____	Odo End	_____
From		To	
Date	_____ / _____ /2016	Total Miles	_____
Odo Start	_____	Odo End	_____
From		To	
Date	_____ / _____ /2016	Total Miles	_____
Odo Start	_____	Odo End	_____
From		To	
Date	_____ / _____ /2016	Total Miles	_____
Odo Start	_____	Odo End	_____
From		To	
Date	_____ / _____ /2016	Total Miles	_____
Odo Start	_____	Odo End	_____
From		To	
Date	_____ / _____ /2016	Total Miles	_____
Odo Start	_____	Odo End	_____
From		To	

Date _____ / _____ /2016	Total Miles _____
Odo Start _____	Odo End _____
From	To
Date _____ / _____ /2016	Total Miles _____
Odo Start _____	Odo End _____
From	To
Date _____ / _____ /2016	Total Miles _____
Odo Start _____	Odo End _____
From	To
Date _____ / _____ /2016	Total Miles _____
Odo Start _____	Odo End _____
From	To
Date _____ / _____ /2016	Total Miles _____
Odo Start _____	Odo End _____
From	To
Date _____ / _____ /2016	Total Miles _____
Odo Start _____	Odo End _____
From	To
Date _____ / _____ /2016	Total Miles _____
Odo Start _____	Odo End _____
From	To
Date _____ / _____ /2016	Total Miles _____
Odo Start _____	Odo End _____
From	To
Date _____ / _____ /2016	Total Miles _____
Odo Start _____	Odo End _____
From	To
Date _____ / _____ /2016	Total Miles _____
Odo Start _____	Odo End _____
From	To
Date _____ / _____ /2016	Total Miles _____
Odo Start _____	Odo End _____
From	To

Date	/	/2016	Total Miles	
Odo Start			Odo End	
From			To	

Date	/	/2016	Total Miles	
Odo Start			Odo End	
From			To	

Date	/	/2016	Total Miles	
Odo Start			Odo End	
From			To	

Date	/	/2016	Total Miles	
Odo Start			Odo End	
From			To	

Date	/	/2016	Total Miles	
Odo Start			Odo End	
From			To	

Date	/	/2016	Total Miles	
Odo Start			Odo End	
From			To	

Date	/	/2016	Total Miles	
Odo Start			Odo End	
From			To	

Date	/	/2016	Total Miles	
Odo Start			Odo End	
From			To	

Date	/	/2016	Total Miles	
Odo Start			Odo End	
From			To	

Date	/	/2016	Total Miles	
Odo Start			Odo End	
From			To	

Date	/	/2016	Total Miles	
Odo Start			Odo End	
From			To	

Date / /2016	Total Miles _____
Odo Start _____	Odo End _____
From _____	To _____
Date / /2016	Total Miles _____
Odo Start _____	Odo End _____
From _____	To _____
Date / /2016	Total Miles _____
Odo Start _____	Odo End _____
From _____	To _____
Date / /2016	Total Miles _____
Odo Start _____	Odo End _____
From _____	To _____
Date / /2016	Total Miles _____
Odo Start _____	Odo End _____
From _____	To _____
Date / /2016	Total Miles _____
Odo Start _____	Odo End _____
From _____	To _____
Date / /2016	Total Miles _____
Odo Start _____	Odo End _____
From _____	To _____
Date / /2016	Total Miles _____
Odo Start _____	Odo End _____
From _____	To _____
Date / /2016	Total Miles _____
Odo Start _____	Odo End _____
From _____	To _____
Date / /2016	Total Miles _____
Odo Start _____	Odo End _____
From _____	To _____
Date / /2016	Total Miles _____
Odo Start _____	Odo End _____
From _____	To _____

Date _____/_____/2016	Total Miles	_____
Odo Start _____	Odo End	_____
From _____	To	_____
Date _____/_____/2016	Total Miles	_____
Odo Start _____	Odo End	_____
From _____	To	_____
Date _____/_____/2016	Total Miles	_____
Odo Start _____	Odo End	_____
From _____	To	_____
Date _____/_____/2016	Total Miles	_____
Odo Start _____	Odo End	_____
From _____	To	_____
Date _____/_____/2016	Total Miles	_____
Odo Start _____	Odo End	_____
From _____	To	_____
Date _____/_____/2016	Total Miles	_____
Odo Start _____	Odo End	_____
From _____	To	_____
Date _____/_____/2016	Total Miles	_____
Odo Start _____	Odo End	_____
From _____	To	_____
Date _____/_____/2016	Total Miles	_____
Odo Start _____	Odo End	_____
From _____	To	_____
Date _____/_____/2016	Total Miles	_____
Odo Start _____	Odo End	_____
From _____	To	_____
Date _____/_____/2016	Total Miles	_____
Odo Start _____	Odo End	_____
From _____	To	_____
Date _____/_____/2016	Total Miles	_____
Odo Start _____	Odo End	_____
From _____	To	_____

Date _____/_____/2016	Total Miles _____
Odo Start _____	Odo End _____
From _____	To _____
Date _____/_____/2016	Total Miles _____
Odo Start _____	Odo End _____
From _____	To _____
Date _____/_____/2016	Total Miles _____
Odo Start _____	Odo End _____
From _____	To _____
Date _____/_____/2016	Total Miles _____
Odo Start _____	Odo End _____
From _____	To _____
Date _____/_____/2016	Total Miles _____
Odo Start _____	Odo End _____
From _____	To _____
Date _____/_____/2016	Total Miles _____
Odo Start _____	Odo End _____
From _____	To _____
Date _____/_____/2016	Total Miles _____
Odo Start _____	Odo End _____
From _____	To _____
Date _____/_____/2016	Total Miles _____
Odo Start _____	Odo End _____
From _____	To _____
Date _____/_____/2016	Total Miles _____
Odo Start _____	Odo End _____
From _____	To _____
Date _____/_____/2016	Total Miles _____
Odo Start _____	Odo End _____
From _____	To _____
Date _____/_____/2016	Total Miles _____
Odo Start _____	Odo End _____
From _____	To _____

Date _____/_____/2016	Total Miles _____
Odo Start _____	Odo End _____
From	To

Date _____/_____/2016	Total Miles _____
Odo Start _____	Odo End _____
From	To

Date _____/_____/2016	Total Miles _____
Odo Start _____	Odo End _____
From	To

Date _____/_____/2016	Total Miles _____
Odo Start _____	Odo End _____
From	To

Date _____/_____/2016	Total Miles _____
Odo Start _____	Odo End _____
From	To

Date _____/_____/2016	Total Miles _____
Odo Start _____	Odo End _____
From	To

Date _____/_____/2016	Total Miles _____
Odo Start _____	Odo End _____
From	To

Date _____/_____/2016	Total Miles _____
Odo Start _____	Odo End _____
From	To

Date _____/_____/2016	Total Miles _____
Odo Start _____	Odo End _____
From	To

Date _____/_____/2016	Total Miles _____
Odo Start _____	Odo End _____
From	To

Date _____/_____/2016	Total Miles _____
Odo Start _____	Odo End _____
From	To

Date	/	/2016	Total Miles	
Odo Start			Odo End	
From			To	

Date	/	/2016	Total Miles	
Odo Start			Odo End	
From			To	

Date	/	/2016	Total Miles	
Odo Start			Odo End	
From			To	

Date	/	/2016	Total Miles	
Odo Start			Odo End	
From			To	

Date	/	/2016	Total Miles	
Odo Start			Odo End	
From			To	

Date	/	/2016	Total Miles	
Odo Start			Odo End	
From			To	

Date	/	/2016	Total Miles	
Odo Start			Odo End	
From			To	

Date	/	/2016	Total Miles	
Odo Start			Odo End	
From			To	

Date	/	/2016	Total Miles	
Odo Start			Odo End	
From			To	

Date	/	/2016	Total Miles	
Odo Start			Odo End	
From			To	

Date	/	/2016	Total Miles	
Odo Start			Odo End	
From			To	

Date _____/_____/2016	Total Miles _____	
Odo Start _____	Odo End _____	
From _____	To _____	
Date _____/_____/2016	Total Miles _____	
Odo Start _____	Odo End _____	
From _____	To _____	
Date _____/_____/2016	Total Miles _____	
Odo Start _____	Odo End _____	
From _____	To _____	
Date _____/_____/2016	Total Miles _____	
Odo Start _____	Odo End _____	
From _____	To _____	
Date _____/_____/2016	Total Miles _____	
Odo Start _____	Odo End _____	
From _____	To _____	
Date _____/_____/2016	Total Miles _____	
Odo Start _____	Odo End _____	
From _____	To _____	
Date _____/_____/2016	Total Miles _____	
Odo Start _____	Odo End _____	
From _____	To _____	
Date _____/_____/2016	Total Miles _____	
Odo Start _____	Odo End _____	
From _____	To _____	
Date _____/_____/2016	Total Miles _____	
Odo Start _____	Odo End _____	
From _____	To _____	
Date _____/_____/2016	Total Miles _____	
Odo Start _____	Odo End _____	
From _____	To _____	
Date _____/_____/2016	Total Miles _____	
Odo Start _____	Odo End _____	
From _____	To _____	

Date _____/_____/2016	Total Miles _____
Odo Start _____	Odo End _____
From	To
Date _____/_____/2016	Total Miles _____
Odo Start _____	Odo End _____
From	To
Date _____/_____/2016	Total Miles _____
Odo Start _____	Odo End _____
From	To
Date _____/_____/2016	Total Miles _____
Odo Start _____	Odo End _____
From	To
Date _____/_____/2016	Total Miles _____
Odo Start _____	Odo End _____
From	To
Date _____/_____/2016	Total Miles _____
Odo Start _____	Odo End _____
From	To
Date _____/_____/2016	Total Miles _____
Odo Start _____	Odo End _____
From	To
Date _____/_____/2016	Total Miles _____
Odo Start _____	Odo End _____
From	To
Date _____/_____/2016	Total Miles _____
Odo Start _____	Odo End _____
From	To
Date _____/_____/2016	Total Miles _____
Odo Start _____	Odo End _____
From	To
Date _____/_____/2016	Total Miles _____
Odo Start _____	Odo End _____
From	To

Date	/	/2016	Total Miles	
Odo Start			Odo End	
From			To	
Date	/	/2016	Total Miles	
Odo Start			Odo End	
From			To	
Date	/	/2016	Total Miles	
Odo Start			Odo End	
From			To	
Date	/	/2016	Total Miles	
Odo Start			Odo End	
From			To	
Date	/	/2016	Total Miles	
Odo Start			Odo End	
From			To	
Date	/	/2016	Total Miles	
Odo Start			Odo End	
From			To	
Date	/	/2016	Total Miles	
Odo Start			Odo End	
From			To	
Date	/	/2016	Total Miles	
Odo Start			Odo End	
From			To	
Date	/	/2016	Total Miles	
Odo Start			Odo End	
From			To	
Date	/	/2016	Total Miles	
Odo Start			Odo End	
From			To	
Date	/	/2016	Total Miles	
Odo Start			Odo End	
From			To	

Date	_____ / _____ /2016	Total Miles	_____
Odo Start	_____	Odo End	_____
From		To	

Date	_____ / _____ /2016	Total Miles	_____
Odo Start	_____	Odo End	_____
From		To	

Date	_____ / _____ /2016	Total Miles	_____
Odo Start	_____	Odo End	_____
From		To	

Date	_____ / _____ /2016	Total Miles	_____
Odo Start	_____	Odo End	_____
From		To	

Date	_____ / _____ /2016	Total Miles	_____
Odo Start	_____	Odo End	_____
From		To	

Date	_____ / _____ /2016	Total Miles	_____
Odo Start	_____	Odo End	_____
From		To	

Date	_____ / _____ /2016	Total Miles	_____
Odo Start	_____	Odo End	_____
From		To	

Date	_____ / _____ /2016	Total Miles	_____
Odo Start	_____	Odo End	_____
From		To	

Date	_____ / _____ /2016	Total Miles	_____
Odo Start	_____	Odo End	_____
From		To	

Date	_____ / _____ /2016	Total Miles	_____
Odo Start	_____	Odo End	_____
From		To	

Date	_____ / _____ /2016	Total Miles	_____
Odo Start	_____	Odo End	_____
From		To	

Date _____/_____/2016	Total Miles _____
Odo Start _____	Odo End _____
From _____	To _____

Date _____/_____/2016	Total Miles _____
Odo Start _____	Odo End _____
From _____	To _____

Date _____/_____/2016	Total Miles _____
Odo Start _____	Odo End _____
From _____	To _____

Date _____/_____/2016	Total Miles _____
Odo Start _____	Odo End _____
From _____	To _____

Date _____/_____/2016	Total Miles _____
Odo Start _____	Odo End _____
From _____	To _____

Date _____/_____/2016	Total Miles _____
Odo Start _____	Odo End _____
From _____	To _____

Date _____/_____/2016	Total Miles _____
Odo Start _____	Odo End _____
From _____	To _____

Date _____/_____/2016	Total Miles _____
Odo Start _____	Odo End _____
From _____	To _____

Date _____/_____/2016	Total Miles _____
Odo Start _____	Odo End _____
From _____	To _____

Date _____/_____/2016	Total Miles _____
Odo Start _____	Odo End _____
From _____	To _____

Date _____/_____/2016	Total Miles _____
Odo Start _____	Odo End _____
From _____	To _____

Date _____/_____/2016	Total Miles _____
Odo Start _____	Odo End _____
From _____	To _____
Date _____/_____/2016	Total Miles _____
Odo Start _____	Odo End _____
From _____	To _____
Date _____/_____/2016	Total Miles _____
Odo Start _____	Odo End _____
From _____	To _____
Date _____/_____/2016	Total Miles _____
Odo Start _____	Odo End _____
From _____	To _____
Date _____/_____/2016	Total Miles _____
Odo Start _____	Odo End _____
From _____	To _____
Date _____/_____/2016	Total Miles _____
Odo Start _____	Odo End _____
From _____	To _____
Date _____/_____/2016	Total Miles _____
Odo Start _____	Odo End _____
From _____	To _____
Date _____/_____/2016	Total Miles _____
Odo Start _____	Odo End _____
From _____	To _____
Date _____/_____/2016	Total Miles _____
Odo Start _____	Odo End _____
From _____	To _____
Date _____/_____/2016	Total Miles _____
Odo Start _____	Odo End _____
From _____	To _____
Date _____/_____/2016	Total Miles _____
Odo Start _____	Odo End _____
From _____	To _____

Date _____/_____/2016	Total Miles _____
Odo Start _____	Odo End _____
From _____	To _____
Date _____/_____/2016	Total Miles _____
Odo Start _____	Odo End _____
From _____	To _____
Date _____/_____/2016	Total Miles _____
Odo Start _____	Odo End _____
From _____	To _____
Date _____/_____/2016	Total Miles _____
Odo Start _____	Odo End _____
From _____	To _____
Date _____/_____/2016	Total Miles _____
Odo Start _____	Odo End _____
From _____	To _____
Date _____/_____/2016	Total Miles _____
Odo Start _____	Odo End _____
From _____	To _____
Date _____/_____/2016	Total Miles _____
Odo Start _____	Odo End _____
From _____	To _____
Date _____/_____/2016	Total Miles _____
Odo Start _____	Odo End _____
From _____	To _____
Date _____/_____/2016	Total Miles _____
Odo Start _____	Odo End _____
From _____	To _____
Date _____/_____/2016	Total Miles _____
Odo Start _____	Odo End _____
From _____	To _____
Date _____/_____/2016	Total Miles _____
Odo Start _____	Odo End _____
From _____	To _____